JEDI ACADEMY

ATTACK OF THE FURBALL

A Christina Starspeeder Story

Jarrett J. Krosoczka & Amy Ignatow

Scholastic Inc.

For Onyx, Azure, and Ember
—Jarrett

To my favorite Wookiee, Dan Lazar
—Amy

Published in the UK by Scholastic Children's Books, 2019
Euston House, 24 Eversholt Street, London NWI IDB
A division of Scholastic Limited

London ~ New York ~ Toronto ~ Sydney ~ Auckland
Mexico City ~ New Delhi ~ Hong Kong

SCHOLASTIC and associated logos are trademarks and/or
registered trademarks of Scholastic Inc.

First published in the US by Scholastic Inc., 2019

ISBN 978 1407 19553 7

A CIP catalogue record for this book is available from the British Library.

Printed by CPI Group (UK) Ltd, Croydon, CR0 4YY
Papers used by Scholastic Children's Books are made from wood grown in sustainable forests.

2 4 6 8 10 9 7 5 3 1

www.starwars.com
www.scholastic.co.uk

HEPTADAY

It feels good to be back on the *Faravahar*! After the mess on Canto Bight, I half expected the Masters would want to keep us off of missions, but I should have known that's not the Jedi way. Do or do not, there is no try. Even after a fight with some Gamorrean guards and a Hutt.

I'm definitely more comfortable now on the *Faravahar* than I was at first, even though I swear Q-13 is really working hard to make sure I don't get too comfortable.

I wonder how Victor is doing on Devaron. He's probably frustrated because the planet is too heavily forested for him to fly a speeder.

And I've heard that his Jedi Master, Iyawa is really impressive and hard to please. Then again, not everyone is as lucky as I am to be perfectly matched with the right Jedi Master.

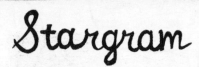

SpeedyC: Got to make sure we can breathe in an emergency!

XelThaKiffar: Food or a building material? #Lunch #Jedha #SendNourishment

BeepBoopBorksmit: @XelThaKiffar Working on it!

Number1Lyndar: So. Close! #MasterMun #SoClose

FrkForce720: We make our own fun! @XelThaKiffar

ProfessorAfos: Swimming with a Krikthasi! #Baralou #HighTide

We talked with a farmer and his family, and it really made me think about how easy it was for us to grow up on Naboo. Victor and I lived really close to other kids, there was water and food everywhere, and everyone got along. On Tatooine, the farm kids maybe see their friends once every week or two, and leaving their communities is really dangerous. If they don't get attacked by Tusken Raiders, they still have to worry about their speeders breaking down in the middle of the desert. If they get stuck somewhere ... that's it for them. Little Cody has never even seen a lake.

My brother and I would go swimming with our Gungan friends every day.

What's swimming?

Youngling, inside.

Christina, look sharp!

Dear Master Ro and Apprentice Christina and grumpy droid,

Thank you so much for defending our farm. I hope one day I can be a Jedi like you and leave Tatooine and go swimming in a lake.

Love,
Cody

That's nice.

Sure. But ... what are the chances of him ever getting off Tatooine? Or of his family being safe from the Tusken Raiders?

There are some things we just can't know.

I HAVE BEEN IN THIS OIL FOR AN HOUR. A FULL HOUR. SOMEBODY GET ME OUT.

DUODAY

What does Master Ro mean, there are some things we just can't know? That seems like a super easy thing to say when bad things happen to good people. What if I gave that as an answer every time anyone asked me a question?

There has to be a better answer.

GALAXY FEED

Mygeeto
Hotspots for
Cold Nights

Goonga the
Hutt Trial
to Begin
Today

Get the
Devaronian
Horned
Glamour!

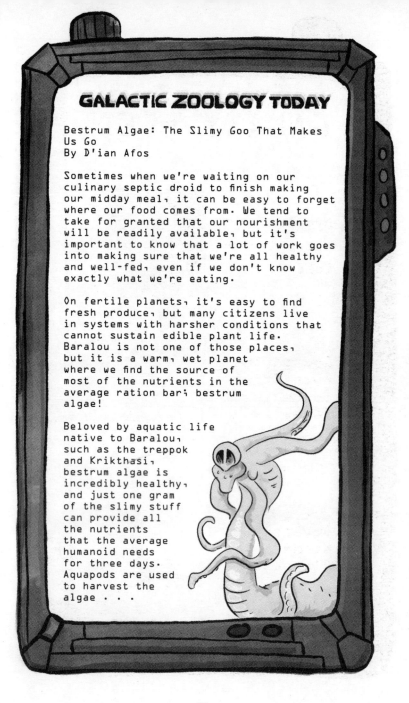

GALACTIC ZOOLOGY TODAY

Bestrum Algae: The Slimy Goo That Makes
Us Go
By D'ian Afos

Sometimes when we're waiting on our
culinary septic droid to finish making
our midday meal, it can be easy to forget
where our food comes from. We tend to
take for granted that our nourishment
will be readily available, but it's
important to know that a lot of work goes
into making sure that we're all healthy
and well-fed, even if we don't know
exactly what we're eating.

On fertile planets, it's easy to find
fresh produce, but many citizens live
in systems with harsher conditions that
cannot sustain edible plant life.
Baralou is not one of those places,
but it is a warm, wet planet
where we find the source of
most of the nutrients in the
average ration bar; bestrum
algae!

Beloved by aquatic life
native to Baralou,
such as the treppok
and Krikthasi,
bestrum algae is
incredibly healthy,
and just one gram
of the slimy stuff
can provide all
the nutrients
that the average
humanoid needs
for three days.
Aquapods are used
to harvest the
algae . . .

Welcome back, apprentices! What have you been up to?

Master Sammeh allowed me to stay here on Jedha so we could fix the culinary septic droid, which is . . . mostly fixed.

Master Ojiee and I went to Umbara to help some workers who were trapped in a doonium mine.

I went with Master Mun to guard a transport ship of dignitaries en route to Rodia.

Master Cor took me to Ord Mantell to warn the Mantellians to stop hunting savrips.

Master Ro and I went to Tatooine to protect some moisture farmers who were under threat from Tusken Raiders.

But we left and now the farmers are defenseless so what was even the point.

One of the senators told me I was adequate!

23

So ... that was a fun class.

What do you mean?

I mean that we're all finally getting to go on interesting missions and all you can do is whine about how something bad might happen to the people you met?

I'm not whining, I'm worried.

You're wallowing.

24

THE DAILY MILLENNIUM

CANTO BIGHT'S *CREATURE CARNAGE* TO BEGIN NEW SHOWS ON HOSNIAN PRIME

Once only accessible to the astronomically well-heeled denizens of Canto Bight, *Creature Carnage* is about to become available to those of us who can't afford a luxury stay on Cantonica. "People were lining up to watch the show," said I'gork Faul, *Creature Carnage*'s director, "and we knew we had a hit on our hands that deserved to be seen by everyone."

Faul's idea to have a live-action version of holochess, the popular holographic game that pits fearsome galactic beasts against each other, had never been done before. "It seemed too dangerous," said Lady Urushiol, the organizer intent on bringing *Carnage* to Hosnian Prime, "but I'gork has some kind of power over these animals. He knows which ones will be perfect for our little theater, and they're just like tiny baby tooka cats when he's around! I'm convinced they're having just as much fun as the audience."

26

31

Hey, little guy. I didn't mean to scare you. Where's your mama?

Are you all alone?

Mew!

Christina, Q–thir has alerted the local authorities and they're on their way to collect the loggers. It's time to go.

Okay, I gotta go, little buddy.

Mew.

QUADDAY

I've been thinking a lot about how the Jedi use the Force to serve and protect the universe, but we're limited in how much we can help. Sure, we can stop the baddies, but then what? What happens to the innocent people and small helpless woodland creatures that we leave behind? I know there's no way to make sure that everyone is okay forever, but sometimes we can do something extra to help, and if we're able to do that something extra, aren't we obligated to do so?

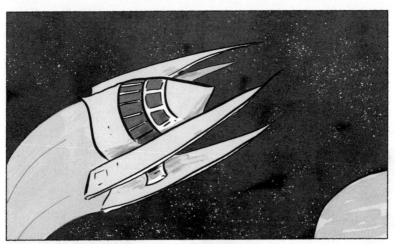

38

Stargram

Number1Lyndar Dorm-mates are INCONSIDERATE.
#NotNamingNames #YouKnowWhoYouAre

SpeedyC: @BeepBoopBorksmit is the best!

XelThaKiffar: No more ration bars! More
of . . . this. #MysteryCube

BeepBoopBorksmit: Introducing Li'l 77!
#DroidLife

LIL77: Welcome to my new Stargram
Account. I am a service droid.
#DroidLife

FrkForce720: Does it ever get warm here?
#JedhaWinter

GALAXY FEED

New Droid
Improv Group
Wins Big at
Intergalactic
Comedy
Symposium

A Rainbow
Lightsaber?
Miners on
Ilum Say It's
Possible

Tour Lady
Urushiol's
Sienar Star
Courier

GALACTIC ZOOLOGY TODAY

Rancors: Vicious Predators or Mouth-
Watering Delicacies?
By D'ian Afos

Ottethan: When people think of this
small, obscure planet a couple of
things come to mind. First, that it
is a wild planet full of unexplored
continents with lush vegetation. But
it would certainly be an interesting
expedition, as the other thing Ottethan
brings to mind is that it is the home
planet to the fierce and terrifying
rancors.

Of course, rancors have been found
on other planets (Felucia, Teth, and
Socorro, to name a few) but the rancors
of Ottethan are rumored to be the
most intelligent as well as the most
deadly. The average rancor measures
five meters tall, weighs approximately
1650 kilograms, and has been known
to swallow humanoids whole (despite
their mouths being full of razor-sharp
fangs), which begs the
question: why would
anybody attempt to
eat one?

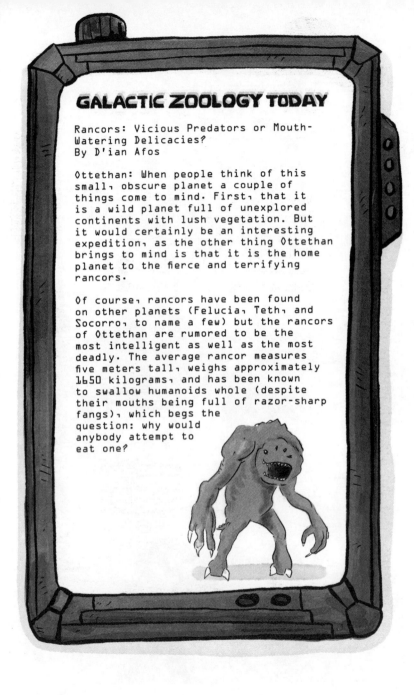

44

JOURNAL

We've been on Bespin for five days now (well, technically we're in Cloud City, an enormous metropolis that floats in Bespin's Life Zone; the one layer of the gas giant's atmosphere that can sustain humanoid life). We've been posing as merchants in order to infiltrate the political elites who might have some intel on the criminals that have been stealing blocks of frozen carbonite filled with processed tibanna gases. Skia Ro is pretty good at blending in; me, not so much.

48

49

MONODAY

After two and a half weeks of constant surveillance and having to figure out new things to wear, we finally have a lead. Master Ro convinced a Barbadelan smuggler that we needed a ship to move some stolen tibanna, and he assumed that we'd purchased the precious gasses from Jobot's brother.

Taking Mobot and his cronies down wasn't easy, mostly due to the fact that we kept apprehending the wrong brother.

52

PENTADAY

We finally got back to Jedha and I raced back to the dormitory to find . . . Fluffernut.

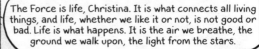
Then what is the point? If we can't be sure about what we're doing, why do we keep doing it?

The Force is life, Christina. It is what connects all living things, and life, whether we like it or not, is not good or bad. Life is what happens. It is the air we breathe, the ground we walk upon, the light from the stars.

Beautiful swoopy capes.

Sure, that too. Life is what we make of it, and as Jedi we are called to do as much as we are able to help others through. Sometimes we are able to do quite a bit. Sometimes we are not. Such is life. Do you understand?

It seems unfair.

No one ever said it would be fair.

Some things are DEFINITELY not fair.

SpeedyC: Super fun cape shopping day!

Number1Lyndar: Swoopless in Jedha.
#irreplaceable #WhyMe

XelThaKiffar: Send. Nourishment.
#RationBarsAreLookingGood

MISSING PREDATORS A CAUSE FOR CONSTERNATION

Two acklays, Tkaczuk and Mr.
Growls, seem to have disappeared
from the Coruscant Intergalactic
Zoo, and noted intergalactic
biologist and columnist Professor
D'ian Afos is concerned.

"I cautioned the zoo board about
keeping and transporting such
dangerous creatures long before
they ever came to Coruscant,"
Professor Afos said, "but there has
always been a public fascination
with dangerous animals, and the
board decided it was worth the
risk. And now they're gone."

"They're not gone," Director
Herkum Bjort told reporters, but
was unable to say exactly where
the carnivorous, bloodthirsty
three-meter tall mix of reptile
and crustacean with razor sharp
teeth and six legs that they use
to spear their prey were located.
"Tkaczuk and Mr. Growls are just
fine. Perhaps Ms. Afos should stick
to doing exposés about banthas."

HEXADAY

There's a meeting of the Jedi High Council this morning, so the rest of us have a rare day off. The others are headed off to tour the Catacombs of Cadera, which sounds really interesting (if kind of creepy), but I've opted to stay behind and have a quiet day in the dorms so I can really focus on being one with the Force.

Okay, I have to stay behind because if I don't, Fluffernut is going to destroy the entire dormitory. She has gotten BIG. I knew she was going to get bigger but this is getting ridiculous. I can't even smuggle her outside anymore to poop! It's a real problem.

Hey, little brother! How's Devaron?

Pretty good, although I'm not sure that Master Iyawa likes me. She's really hard to impress.

You have to stop trying to impress her. They always know when you're being a try-hard.

But she's not letting me do anything cool!

Don't worry, I used to feel the same with Master Ro but now she trusts me. Don't worry—

CHRISTINA! BEHIND YOU! THERE'S A NEXU BEHIND YOU, GET YOUR LIGHTSABER!!!

Christina, it was such a bummer that you couldn't come.

Lyndar, what are you looking at?

A Stargram with a photo of a nexu that shows how big Christina's mistake is going to get.

What's up, furrybutt? You look—GAH!

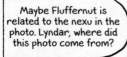

Maybe Fluffernut is related to the nexu in the photo. Lyndar, where did this photo come from?

A Stargram account from my friend who is traveling through Utapau.

Q–13! How lovely to see you!

Really? Why?

Oh, just because I was hoping you'd be able to help me with the culinary septic droid.

No, thank you, it looks like it was attacked by a wild animal. You're on your own.

Christina?

Yes, Q–13?

Skia Ro needs you to run to the market station to get some power converters.

73

GALAXY FEED

Master Yoda's Favorite Stew Recipe

Acklay vs. Rancor: Who Would Win In Hand-to-Claw Combat?

Be Your Own Kyber Crystal

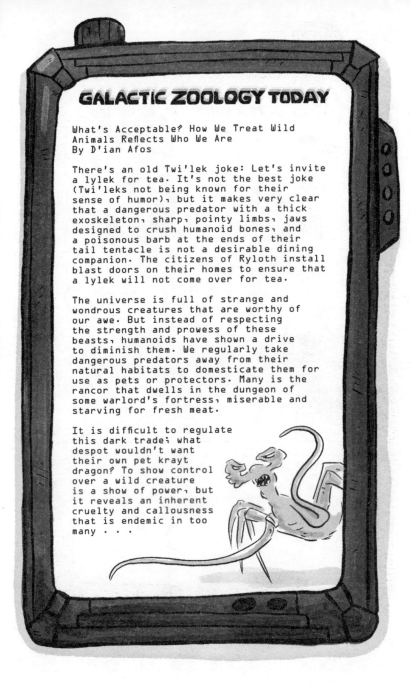

GALACTIC ZOOLOGY TODAY

What's Acceptable? How We Treat Wild
Animals Reflects Who We Are
By D'ian Afos

There's an old Twi'lek joke: Let's invite
a lylek for tea. It's not the best joke
(Twi'leks not being known for their
sense of humor), but it makes very clear
that a dangerous predator with a thick
exoskeleton, sharp, pointy limbs, jaws
designed to crush humanoid bones, and
a poisonous barb at the ends of their
tail tentacle is not a desirable dining
companion. The citizens of Ryloth install
blast doors on their homes to ensure that
a lylek will not come over for tea.

The universe is full of strange and
wondrous creatures that are worthy of
our awe. But instead of respecting
the strength and prowess of these
beasts, humanoids have shown a drive
to diminish them. We regularly take
dangerous predators away from their
natural habitats to domesticate them for
use as pets or protectors. Many is the
rancor that dwells in the dungeon of
some warlord's fortress, miserable and
starving for fresh meat.

It is difficult to regulate
this dark trade; what
despot wouldn't want
their own pet krayt
dragon? To show control
over a wild creature
is a show of power, but
it reveals an inherent
cruelty and callousness
that is endemic in too
many · · ·

Are you all right, Master Ro?

I'gork's apprenticeship did not end well, and lately I have been sensing his presence. I must meditate to discern whether I am feeling a true disturbance in the Force or simply an unwanted memory triggered by the scent of the blartree blossom.

What happened between you two?

The bond between a master and Padawan is sacred, and honesty is of the utmost importance. There can be no secrets. I'gork was full of dark secrets. You must always be honest with me, Christina, even if you think I won't like it.

Yes, Master Ro.

QUADDAY

Skia Ro looked so hurt when she was talking about her former apprentice (or, at least she looked mildly bothered, which is about as much emotion as I've ever seen her show). I need to know what he did that was so bad. Clearly it had to be some real dark side stuff, right? It couldn't be something small, like maybe concealing the fact that he might have saved a wild animal from certain death by sneaking it off of its home planet and then keeping it in his dormitory room until became the size of a landspeeder, could it?

I need to tell her about Fluffernut. She's going to be so disappointed in me. And then what will happen next? Will she be taken away?

79

VICT-orious: Getting around, Devaron-style! #ForestLife #VineBridge

FrkForce720: Send help.

LIL77: I am now a dancing droid. Behold my smooth moves. #DroidLife

Every day Fluffernut gets bigger and it's getting harder to find food for her, especially now that Xel has taken over the kitchen with his cooking experiments.

Here, girl, look at what Xel made for you!

What do nexu know about fine dining anyway.

Apparently a lot.

BLECH!

What?

Nothing!

I know I have to tell Skia Ro about
Fluffernut but that will mean having to
say good-bye to her. And I really, really
don't want to say good-bye.

GALAXY FEED

Hyperdrive: Can We Go Faster? This Corellian Designer Says Probably

New Hosnian Prime Hotspots!

Mystery Wild Animal Goes on Destructive Rampage in NiJedha Marketplace

GALACTIC ZOOLOGY TODAY

Caring For Your Kaadu
By D'ian Afos

Long beloved by the natives of Naboo, a
tamed kaadu is a staple of Gungan life.
It is said that a Gungan without a kaadu
is like a Jedi without a lightsaber, and
it is a rite of passage for a young Gungan
to tame their kaadu.

A kaadu is primarily used for
transportation, both in and out of the
water. But the kaadu are so much more than
mere beasts of burden; they are companions
to their Gungan counterparts, and when
treated with affection and respect will
respond in kind. And every good kaadu
companion knows that what kaadus love
most is moisture.

They love mud! They love swamps! They love
taking long, leisurely swims, and can
remain underwater for up to two hours. To
deny your kaadu constant access to water
is to show your kaadu that their well-
being is not your concern, and don't be
too surprised to find that this tame animal
is willing to buck you off their back the
moment a pool comes into view . . .

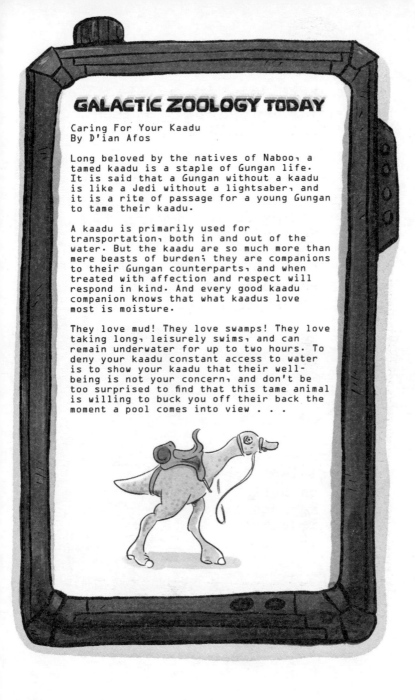

I still don't know what to do with Fluffernut.
She's too young to go back into the wild, and
besides, there isn't really a wild on Jedha to
take her to, just a lot of cold desert.

But I do have until the end of the week
to figure it out, which is good because all
the apprentices have just been called out
to missions. It's a little weird, as we rarely
all go away on missions at the same time
(certainly not at the same moment). Kyt
seems confident that Li'l 77 can watch over
Fluffernut, as long as there aren't any
fires.

Are you
packing just
regular robes?

I guess so?

We will be guarding the Royal Palace of Alderaan.

Is the royal family under threat?

No, they're hosting . . . a concert. Axi Nue and the Borken Hoopstirs.

Oh. Is it really necessary that we be there?

We are Jedi. We go where we are needed.

Do we at least get to go to the concert?

No.

Stargram

SpeedyC: Thought I almost saw Axi Nue! But it was just a fan dressed like Axi Nue. #Alderaan

XelThaKiffar: So glad I got to come to Marfa to collect Pulsifarian moss. This seems like a great use of my time. #Sarcasm

BeepBoopBorksmit: Good thing I'm here to guard this container transport from pirates who love polta beans. #MusicalFruit

96

98

Someone stole Fluffernut! But who? And why? And is she even still alive? Frk thinks that she was probably just given a tranquilizer. When she wakes up she's going to be so scared. I'm so scared. What am I going to do?

I know I have to tell Skia Ro. I guess this is the end of Jedi Academy...

103

I showed Master Ro the footage of
Fluffernut being nexu-napped and she was
very disturbed. She then told me more
about I'gork Faul, her old apprentice. He'd
been really strong with the Force, but
despite that he'd quit his apprenticeship
and left Jedha. Master Ro made it sound
like he didn't really leave on good terms.
(I didn't ask but I'm pretty sure they're
not exchanging Life Day greetings.)

And the creep who
took Fluffernut?
Master Ro is certain
it's I'gork Faul.

Master Ro said she doesn't know exactly
what he's been up to since they parted
ways, but she heard rumors over the years
that he was smuggling weapons, stealing
technology, and rigging elections.

The good news is that it looks like we're going to do something to find Fluffernut. Skia Ro and the other Masters have called an emergency meeting which we all must attend. Rumor has it that someone from the High Council will be there as well, which means this I'gork Faul guy's involvement is pretty serious.

The bad news is that Fluffernut has been abducted by a former apprentice whose powers are formidable enough to bring one of the members of the High Council to Jedha. What is he planning on doing with Fluffernut?

The other good news is that I haven't been kicked out of my apprenticeship . . . yet. But Master Ro is not happy with me.

Apprentices, as you well know, one of your own has been keeping a dangerous nexu in the apprentice dormitory. She did not have permission to take the beast from its planet, nor did she have permission to keep it as a pet.

Fluffernut isn't really dangerous, just irritating.

You have also been made aware that a former Jedi apprentice, I'gork Faul, is responsible for abducting the juvenile nexu from the dormitory.

For some time, we have been monitoring a nefarious gambling ring that has set its sights on animal shows. Wild creatures are being pitted against each other to do violent combat for the amusement of audiences.

Like in *Creature Carnage*?

Exactly, only they claim that no animals get hurt during those fights and that it's all for show.

We believe that there are other, bloodier, secret *Creature Carnage* bouts available to a smaller audience of illegal gamblers. And I'gork Faul is most definitely involved.

Oh no!

Uhmahgosh he spoke to me!

To Utapau we will go. Free and collect the beasts the Jedi Masters will. Apprentices observe, and help when time it is for us to return the creatures to their home planets.

Do you think the animals are going to be all right?

What is being done to them is a great evil. But we have consulted with Professor D'ian Afros, who has given us tranquilizers to subdue them. We will do our best to rescue them and reintegrate them into their home environments.

Work together, we will, to end this.

Apprentices, return to your dormitory to pack your necessities and meet your Masters at their ships. You leave in half an hour.

HEPTADAY

I've just learned that Master Yoda will be flying in the Faravahar with us! I'm so worried about Fluffernut and I still don't know what's going to happen to me when all of this is over, but at least I'll get to spend time with Master Yoda. Even if it is the last time I ever get to do that. I really don't want to think about that. Oh no, what if it's the last time I ever get to be with my favorite teacher? I never imagined things would get so messed up.

As we were packing to go, Lyndar brought me the cape that Fluffernut had mauled, and said that he wanted to give it to Fluffernut to keep if we were able to find her. I could see all of her little teeth marks and the whole thing was still encrusted with her drool, which was kind of disgusting but also made me burst into tears. She was so destructive. I miss her so much!

The Empyrean
Drongo

The Cosmic
Chickadee

The Chandrilan
Sparrowhawk

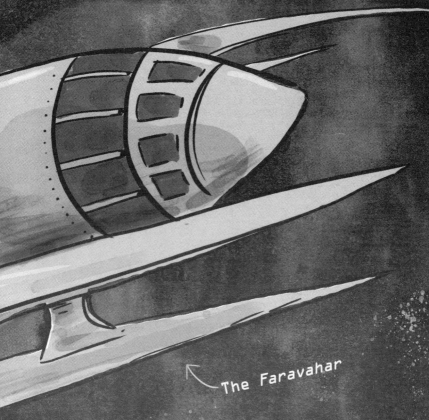

The Hoatzin

The Faravahar

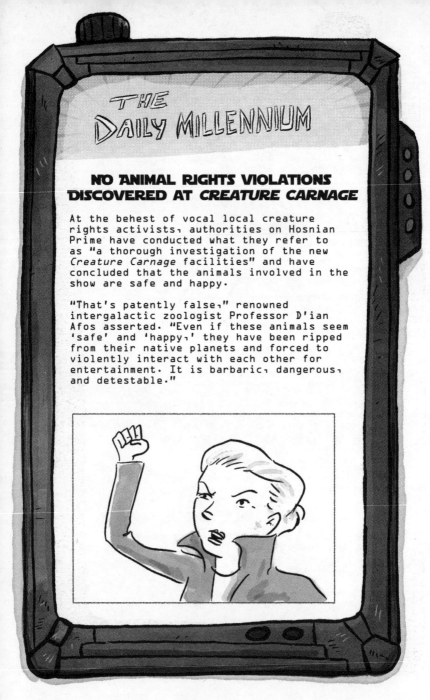

THE DAILY MILLENNIUM

NO ANIMAL RIGHTS VIOLATIONS DISCOVERED AT *CREATURE CARNAGE*

At the behest of vocal local creature rights activists, authorities on Hosnian Prime have conducted what they refer to as "a thorough investigation of the new *Creature Carnage* facilities" and have concluded that the animals involved in the show are safe and happy.

"That's patently false," renowned intergalactic zoologist Professor D'ian Afos asserted. "Even if these animals seem 'safe' and 'happy,' they have been ripped from their native planets and forced to violently interact with each other for entertainment. It is barbaric, dangerous, and detestable."

Lady Urushiol, a major investor in
Creature Carnage, disagrees with Afos'
assessment. "Like most people who
over-identify with animals, Professor
Afos is a kook who probably needs
a friend. Our animals are safe and
happy, as are our audiences. And every
Pentaday is One Cred Deep-Fried Nuna
Leg Night!"

Despite assurances from the
inspectors, the creature rights
activists insist . . .

Master Ro gave me an article about Utapau to read, and of all the places we've been since I became her apprentice, this definitely looks like the least pleasant one. It's a desert planet like Jedha and Tatooine, but there's something about it that feels very different. Wrong.

Skia telling Q-13 off was my favorite thing ever.

MONODAY

We've arrived at our lodgings and the Masters have told us to rest while Master Ojiee meets with his informant. It's a really nice hotel, but I'm still feeling incredibly uneasy.

Masters Ro, Sammeh, Cor, Ojiee, Mun, and Yoda gathered us together for one final meeting before they left to find the animals. Their instructions to us were pretty clear.

125

Number1Lyndar: Dance party! @BeepBoopBorksmit @XelThaKiffar #ShakeIt

XelThaKiffar: What should I use to break this?

Number1Lyndar: Change of scenery! #LobbyStyle

I keep thinking about what Yoda said;
that the Force flows through all of us
and connects all of us. Master Ro felt
I'gork Faul's presence. Maybe if I try
I could sense Fluffernut's? I need to
know if she's all right.

Christina! Where are you going?

I was trying to use the power of the Force to find Fluffernut and I had a vision that the masters were about to walk into a trap!

That's messed up.

We have to help them!

Hold your fathiers, Christo. Think for a second. Even if the masters were walking into a trap, they could totally handle it.

But . . .

Thank you for seeing me, Tulpehoc.

I do not have time for this, right now, Keith. Especially after your monumental failure on Cholganna.

But I can make up for it. I have information on the whereabouts of the Jedi!

You have no new information. As we speak they are approaching our trap. They will be dealt with momentarily.

But there are more of them! Their apprentices are still at the hotel, did you know that?

They are children who will be easy to defeat.

Please, Tulpehoc, what can I do to get back in Urushiol's good graces?

Be less pathetic.

Mee-yowch.

138

We do?

Yeah, I was taking a video of the conversation over my shoulder the whole time.

Really? I thought you were just taking more selfies.

In that lighting? Don't make me guffaw.

Once the others saw Lyndar's video, they finally believed me.

I'd like to say that I wasn't at all smug about having been proven totally right, but I will say that if something like this ever happens again I'll have no problem saying, "Remember that time I was totally right and no one believed me because you nerf herders all thought I was unable to separate my emotions from the task at hand? REMEMBER THAT? YEAH. I THOUGHT YOU DID."

We all rushed out without even cleaning up the room service to cover our tracks.

I've never been to any sort of massive event before—the closest I've ever come was guarding the Axi Nue and the Borken Hoopstirs concert, and I didn't even get to go inside, so I didn't know what to expect. It was huge, and pretty grimy, and full of the type of people who pay money to see innocent creatures tearing each other apart. They were . . . unfriendly.

Everyone was loud and obnoxious and impatient for the battles to begin. I know we were trying to blend in but it was hard to keep the disgust off of my face. Why do people like these sorts of things? I don't think I'll ever understand.

Frk found an entrance to what looked like either a bathroom or the lower levels of the arena, and one by one we were able to sneak in without anyone noticing. And we thought the upper level smelled bad!

150

Well . . . this was unexpected. No matter. RELEASE THE BEASTS!

HARM THEM DO NOT!

KRSSH!

TRIDAY

It took some effort, but we were able to load all of the sedated creatures into the Jedi ships and now we're taking them home. Fluffernut immediately curled up with the other nexu. It has to be her real mom—I'gork Faul must have taken her from Cholganna not long before we showed up to stop the illegal loggers. I'm going to name her Smooshface.

Terrible at naming creatures, you are. Really. Stop, you must.

Because we're heading back to Cholganna, we're also taking Keith the Logger. This time he won't escape the Cholgannian authorities, although he won't stop talking about how we were never going to find I'gork Faul. According to Keith, Master Ro's old apprentice has illegal operations all over the galaxy. It feels so creepy to know he's still out there. But I guess that's why I want to be a Jedi Knight—to stop people like I'gork Faul.

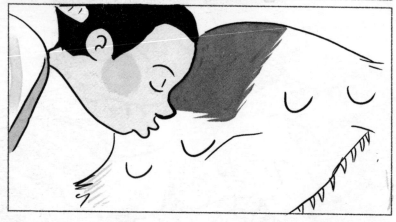

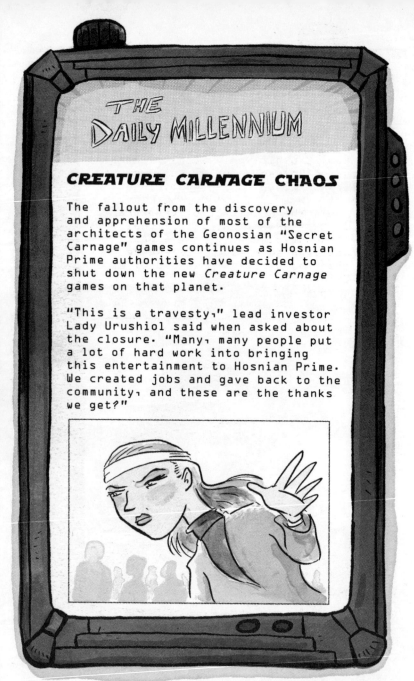

THE DAILY MILLENNIUM

CREATURE CARNAGE CHAOS

The fallout from the discovery and apprehension of most of the architects of the Geonosian "Secret Carnage" games continues as Hosnian Prime authorities have decided to shut down the new *Creature Carnage* games on that planet.

"This is a travesty," lead investor Lady Urushiol said when asked about the closure. "Many, many people put a lot of hard work into bringing this entertainment to Hosnian Prime. We created jobs and gave back to the community, and these are the thanks we get?"

But when confronted about the whereabouts of her erstwhile business partner, I'gork Faul, Lady Urushiol only said, "I hardly know the man, and if you'll excuse me, I'm late for an appointment."

Faul, the architect of *Creature Carnage* as well as its illegal offshoot, *Secret Carnage*, has not been seen since his escape from the battle with the Jedi at Utapau.

After we left Cholganna, Master Ro called me into her quarters. I was all set to make my case for remaining her apprentice, but she surprised me.

Stargram

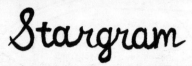

SpeedyC: Heading back to Naboo for a quick break with my squadron! @FrkForce720 @ BeepBoopBorksmit #NabooVacay

XelThaKiffar: So glad to be spending a few days at home! #Kiffu #nom

BeepBoopBorksmit: Do droids get spacesick? Asking for a friend.

Number1Lyndar: Finally got a pic with my Master! #MasterMun #LookinFoine #BlurryPic

LIL77: Droids do not get spacesick. There is merely a glitch in my balance function. #DroidLife #PleaseFixMe #Immediately

VICT-orious: @SpeedyC is coming home today! #BigSurprise

YEARBOOK

Christina Starspeeder
Best Intentioned

Frk Khr Drn
Most Likely to be
One with the Force

Lyndar Syrush
Best Impression of a Kaadu

Kyt Borksmit
Most Likely to Accidentally
Invent a Monster Droid

SUPERLATIVES

Xel Chardin
Pickiest Eater

Yarael Poof
Future Turtleneck Model

Yoda
Cameo, Best

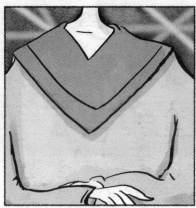

Yarael Poof
Headmasteriest

Jarrett J. Krosoczka is a *New York Times* bestselling author, a two-time winner of the Children's Choice Book Award for the Third to Fourth Grade Book of the Year, an Eisner award nominee, and is the author and/or illustrator of dozens books for young readers. His work includes several picture books, the *Lunch Lady* graphic novels, and *Platypus Police Squad* middle-grade novel series. His graphic memoir, *Hey, Kiddo,* was a National Book Award Finalist.

Jarrett lives in western Massachusetts with his wife and children, and their pugs, Ralph and Frank.

Amy Ignatow is the author and illustrator of The Popularity Papers series and the Odds series. She lives in Philadelphia with her family and really, really wants a lightsaber.